CHECKERBOARD BIOGRAPHY LIBRARY

U.S. PRESIDENTS

The
United States Presidents

JOHN F. KENNEDY

ABDO Publishing Company

Megan M. Gunderson

visit us at
www.abdopublishing.com

Published by ABDO Publishing Company, 8000 West 78th Street, Edina, Minnesota 55439.
Copyright © 2009 by Abdo Consulting Group, Inc. International copyrights reserved in all
countries. No part of this book may be reproduced in any form without written permission from the
publisher. The Checkerboard Library™ is a trademark and logo of ABDO Publishing Company.

Printed in the United States.

Cover Photo: John F. Kennedy Presidential Library and Museum
Interior Photos: Alamy p. 9; AP Images pp. 5, 11, 14, 19, 27; Getty Images pp. 10, 28; iStockphoto
    pp. 29, 32; John F. Kennedy Presidential Library and Museum pp. 9, 13, 16, 21, 23, 24, 25, 26

Editor: BreAnn Rumsch
Art Direction & Cover Design: Neil Klinepier
Interior Design: Neil Klinepier

Library of Congress Cataloging-in-Publication Data

Gunderson, Megan M., 1981-
  John F. Kennedy / Megan M. Gunderson.
      p. cm. -- (The United States presidents)
  Includes index.
  ISBN 978-1-60453-463-4
  1. Kennedy, John F. (John Fitzgerald), 1917-1963--Juvenile literature. 2. Presidents--United
States--Biography--Juvenile literature. I. Title.

  E842.Z9G86 2009
  973.922092--dc22
    [B]
                              2008027038

CONTENTS

JOHN F. KENNEDY

John F. Kennedy was the thirty-fifth U.S. president. He was the youngest man ever elected to the office. Kennedy was also the first Roman Catholic president.

During **World War II**, Kennedy served in the U.S. Navy. He was awarded two medals, including one for heroism. In 1946, Kennedy was elected to the U.S. House of Representatives. Six years later, he was elected to the U.S. Senate. In 1960, the **Democrats** nominated Kennedy to run for president. In a close race, he won the election.

Kennedy took office at a difficult time. America was fighting against the spread of Communism throughout the world. Kennedy took responsibility for the failed Bay of Pigs invasion in Cuba. Then, he successfully led the country through the Cuban **missile** crisis.

President Kennedy never finished his first term. On November 22, 1963, Kennedy was **assassinated** in Dallas, Texas. His vice

president, Lyndon
B. Johnson,
became the new
president. Johnson
carried out many
of Kennedy's plans
for the country.
Meanwhile, the
world mourned
the loss of
this intelligent,
energetic leader.

TIMELINE

1917 - On May 29, John Fitzgerald Kennedy was born in Brookline, Massachusetts.

1935 - Kennedy graduated from Choate School.

1940 - Kennedy's first book, *Why England Slept*, was published; Kennedy graduated from Harvard University.

1943 - In August, Kennedy secured the rescue of his naval crew after their boat, *PT-109*, sank.

1946 - Kennedy was elected to the U.S. House of Representatives.

1952 - Kennedy was elected to the U.S. Senate.

1953 - On September 12, Kennedy married Jacqueline Lee "Jackie" Bouvier.

1957 - Kennedy won a Pulitzer Prize for his book *Profiles in Courage*; on November 27, Kennedy's daughter, Caroline, was born.

1960 - Kennedy was elected the thirty-fifth U.S. president; on November 25, Kennedy's son John Jr. was born.

1961 - In March, Kennedy established the Peace Corps; the Bay of Pigs invasion failed; Kennedy created the Alliance for Progress.

1962 - Kennedy handled the Cuban missile crisis.

1963 - On August 5, the United States signed the Nuclear Test-Ban Treaty; on August 7, Kennedy's son Patrick was born; Lee Harvey Oswald assassinated John F. Kennedy in Dallas, Texas, on November 22.

DID YOU KNOW?

John F. Kennedy was the youngest person elected U.S. president. However, Theodore Roosevelt was the youngest ever to serve as president. Roosevelt became the twenty-sixth U.S. president in 1901. He was a few months younger than Kennedy when he took office after William McKinley's assassination.

After President Kennedy's assassination, several buildings were created or renamed in his honor. New York's Idlewild Airport was renamed John F. Kennedy International Airport on December 10, 1963. The same year, NASA's site in Florida became the John F. Kennedy Space Center. Later, Congress approved funds to create the John F. Kennedy Center for the Performing Arts in Washington, D.C. It opened in 1971.

Senator Kennedy almost became the vice presidential nominee for the 1956 election. Instead, Tennessee senator Estes Kefauver became Adlai E. Stevenson's running mate. The pair lost the election.

PRESIDENT OF THE
POTUS
UNITED STATES

A YOUNG KENNEDY

John Fitzgerald Kennedy was born on May 29, 1917, in Brookline, Massachusetts. His family called him Jack. Jack's parents were Joseph Patrick Kennedy and Rose Fitzgerald Kennedy. At the age of 25, Joseph had become a bank president. Over the years, he made his fortune in the **stock market**. Rose's father had been the mayor of Boston, Massachusetts.

Joseph and Rose married in 1914. Jack was the second of their nine children. He had one older brother, Joseph Jr. Jack's younger brothers and sisters were Rosemary, Kathleen, Eunice, Patricia, Robert, Jean, and Edward.

Religion, sports, and competition were a big part of the Kennedy children's lives. Joseph Jr. dominated the family activities. Already he was preparing for a political career.

FAST FACTS

BORN - May 29, 1917
WIFE - Jacqueline Lee "Jackie" Bouvier (1929–1994)
CHILDREN - 3
POLITICAL PARTY - Democrat
AGE AT INAUGURATION - 43
YEARS SERVED - 1961–1963
VICE PRESIDENT - Lyndon B. Johnson
DIED - November 22, 1963, age 46

8

Jack spent his earliest years in Brookline, a suburb of Boston.

The Kennedy children spent their summers at Hyannis Port, Massachusetts. Today, the family still owns several homes there.

Jack attended private schools in New York and Connecticut. His father encouraged him to play sports. But Jack did not stand out as an athlete. Growing up, he was often sick. In 1935, Jack graduated from Choate School. He had been an average student. Yet Jack was voted "most likely to succeed."

That summer, Jack went to England. There, he studied at the London School of **Economics**. He then entered Princeton University in Princeton, New Jersey. However, he became sick and had to return home.

In autumn 1936, Jack entered Harvard University in Cambridge, Massachusetts. There, he tried again to succeed in

At Harvard, Jack loved studying history, government, and current events.

Jack (left) *and Joseph Jr.* (right) *both traveled the world observing important events for their father* (center).

sports. Unfortunately, Jack hurt his back while playing football. However, he improved as a student.

    Jack's father became ambassador to Great Britain in 1937. So, the Kennedy family moved to London. During the summers, Jack worked for his father. He often visited other countries. He talked with political leaders and observed important events. Then, he reported what he had seen to his father.

WORLD WAR II HERO

In 1939, Kennedy returned to Harvard for his senior year. That year, **World War II** began. At Harvard, Kennedy wrote an important paper. It was about why Great Britain had been unprepared for the war.

Kennedy expanded the work into a book called *Why England Slept*. His father published and promoted the book in 1940. It became a best seller.

That year, Kennedy graduated from Harvard. Then, he studied at Stanford University Graduate School of Business in Stanford, California. He also traveled to several Latin American countries.

Kennedy volunteered to join the U.S. Army in 1941. But, they rejected him because of his weak back. Kennedy spent the summer strengthening his back. That fall, he joined the U.S. Navy.

In 1943, Kennedy took command of a boat called *PT-109*. On the night of August 2, a Japanese destroyer rammed and sank the boat. Lieutenant Kennedy reinjured his back during the attack.

Still, he and his crew swam three miles (5 km) to an island. Kennedy pulled an injured man along as he swam.

Several days later, Kennedy secured their rescue. For the injuries he received, Kennedy was awarded the Purple Heart. He also received the Navy and Marine Corps Medal for his courage and leadership.

Kennedy then returned to the United States. In 1944, he had back surgery. The following year, he left the military. For a while, he worked as a newspaper reporter.

Kennedy served in the U.S. Navy from 1941 to 1945.

Joseph Jr. had died in the war in 1944. After his death, Kennedy became the family's political focus. So, Kennedy set aside **journalism**. He returned to Boston to prepare for his new career.

CONGRESS

Kennedy's younger brother Robert (right) *was his campaign manager in 1952. Later, Robert became U.S. attorney general under President Kennedy.*

In 1946, Kennedy ran for a seat in the U.S. House of Representatives. His family helped him campaign.

Kennedy's opponents accused him of being too wealthy, too young, and too inexperienced. However, Kennedy used these qualities as positive ways to promote himself. The campaign was a success. Kennedy easily won the election.

Congressman Kennedy served on the Education and Labor Committee. He supported low-cost housing. And, he supported higher wages.

Kennedy also backed the Truman Doctrine and the Marshall Plan. Both programs provided **economic** support to various European countries. In this way, they aimed to help stop the spread of Communism.

In 1947, Kennedy became very sick on a trip to England. His doctors told him he had **Addison's disease**. Over the years, the illness would continue to affect him. However, he took medicine to control it. In 1948 and 1950, he easily won reelection to the House.

Kennedy met Jacqueline Lee "Jackie" Bouvier in 1951. She was from a wealthy family and was well educated. Jackie worked as a newspaper photographer and reporter. Kennedy found her intelligence and sense of humor appealing.

In 1952, Kennedy decided to run for the U.S. Senate. Once again, he campaigned hard with his family's help. Kennedy defeated Henry Cabot Lodge Jr. by more than 70,000 votes.

Senator Kennedy helped pass several laws that were important to Massachusetts. He also supported the opening of the Saint Lawrence Seaway. It connected the Great Lakes to the Atlantic Ocean. Kennedy fought to keep the Electoral College. And, he focused on improving **civil rights**.

Kennedy also served on the Senate Committee on Foreign Relations. He supported increasing aid to developing nations in Asia and Africa.

On September 12, 1953, Kennedy married Jackie. They welcomed their daughter, Caroline, on November 27, 1957. A son, John Jr., arrived

The Kennedys often spent time at the Kennedy family home in Hyannis Port. It became known as the summer White House.

on November 25, 1960. They had another son, Patrick, on August 7, 1963. Sadly, he died just two days later.

Meanwhile, Kennedy was still suffering from back problems. He had back operations in October 1954 and February 1955. Kennedy remained in bed for six months.

While he rested, Kennedy decided to write a book. He had been thinking about it for years. *Profiles in Courage* is about eight of the most courageous U.S. senators. It was published in 1956 and quickly became a best seller. The book earned Kennedy the 1957 **Pulitzer Prize** for biography.

By 1957, Kennedy was already thinking about becoming president of the United States. He began by winning reelection to his U.S. Senate seat in 1958.

Kennedy won by nearly 1 million votes! This was the biggest victory in Massachusetts history. The huge win proved Kennedy's popularity.

THE 1960 ELECTION

In January 1960, Kennedy announced his candidacy for U.S. president. He campaigned throughout the year. His younger brothers, Robert and Edward, helped run the campaign. Jackie made public appearances and wrote articles. Kennedy's father provided an airplane for campaign travel.

Kennedy easily won the **Democratic** nomination. Texas senator Lyndon B. Johnson became his **running mate**. The **Republicans** nominated Richard Nixon as their presidential candidate. Nixon was the current U.S. vice president. His running mate was Kennedy's former Senate opponent Henry Cabot Lodge Jr.

In autumn 1960, Kennedy and Nixon met for a series of **debates**. For the first time in U.S. history, the debates were shown on television. As many as 85 to 120 million Americans watched them. Nixon spoke well. Yet Kennedy appeared comfortable, youthful, and energetic on camera. Viewers felt Kennedy had won the debates.

The 1960 presidential election was one of the closest in U.S. history. Nearly 69 million people voted. Kennedy defeated Nixon by fewer than 120,000 **popular votes**. He was elected the thirty-fifth U.S. president.

Kennedy and Johnson received 303 electoral votes to Nixon and Lodge's 219 votes.

THE NEW FRONTIER

President Kennedy's **inauguration** took place on January 20, 1961. In his speech, he announced plans to confront "tyranny, poverty, disease, and war."

When Kennedy had accepted the **Democratic** nomination, he had referred to a New Frontier. As president, his plans soon became known by this name. Congress approved several of President Kennedy's plans. They included higher wages and aid for the poor.

Kennedy also wanted to put an American on the moon before 1970. During this time, America was involved in the **Cold War**. The nation's enemy was the Communist Soviet Union.

In 1961, the Soviets had put a man in space one month before the Americans did. Now, the United States wanted to beat the Soviet Union to the moon. This competition became known as the space race.

Another new Kennedy plan was the Peace Corps. This program sends American volunteers to help developing countries. It was established in March 1961.

John Glenn (right) *commanded the* Friendship 7. *In it, he became the first U.S. astronaut to orbit Earth.*

President Kennedy also wanted to create laws to stop **segregation** and **discrimination**. In June 1963, he proposed **civil rights** legislation to Congress. However, it did not pass until after his death.

21

Foreign relations immediately became an important issue for President Kennedy. America wanted to stop the spread of Communism. Before Kennedy took office, the Central Intelligence Agency had trained anticommunist Cubans. They planned to invade Cuba and help overthrow its leader, Fidel Castro.

In April 1961, they invaded at the Bay of Pigs. However, Castro's army captured most of the invaders. President Kennedy traded food and medicine for the prisoners. He also accepted the blame for the failed Bay of Pigs invasion.

Kennedy feared that many Latin American countries might also become Communist. To prevent this, he created the Alliance for Progress. It provided U.S. aid to Latin American countries so they would not turn to Communism. All Latin American countries except Cuba signed the agreement in August 1961.

Kennedy had more problems with Communism in Germany. In August 1961, the Berlin Wall was built between East and West Berlin. It was meant to stop people in Communist East Berlin from fleeing to West Berlin.

China, another Communist nation, invaded India in 1962. So, President Kennedy sent weapons to India's army. At the same time, South Vietnam was fighting Communist North Vietnam. Kennedy sent thousands of U.S. military advisers to help the South Vietnamese.

PRESIDENT KENNEDY'S CABINET

JANUARY 20, 1961–
NOVEMBER 22, 1963

- **STATE –** Dean Rusk
- **TREASURY –** C. Douglas Dillon
- **DEFENSE –** Robert S. McNamara
- **ATTORNEY GENERAL –** Robert F. Kennedy
- **INTERIOR –** Stewart L. Udall
- **AGRICULTURE –** Orville L. Freeman
- **COMMERCE –** Luther H. Hodges
- **LABOR –** Arthur J. Goldberg
    W. Willard Wirtz (from September 25, 1962)
- **HEALTH, EDUCATION, AND WELFARE –**
    Abraham A. Ribicoff
    Anthony J. Celebrezze (from July 31, 1962)

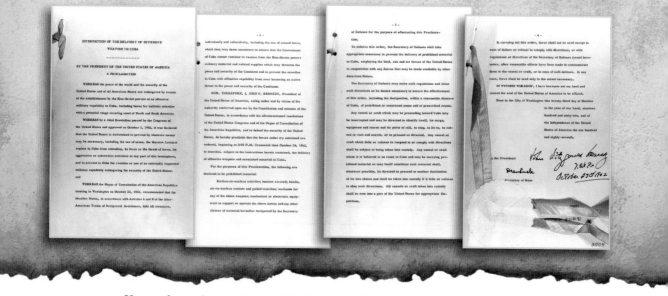

Kennedy authorized the U.S. Navy to block Cuba from Soviet ships.

In October 1962, Kennedy saw important photographs. They were of nuclear **missile** bases under construction in Cuba. He wanted to stop Soviet ships from delivering supplies. So, he announced that the U.S. Navy would block Cuba's coast.

Soviet leader Nikita S. Khrushchev warned President Kennedy against this plan. He said the Soviet Union would defend its shipping rights. A nuclear war could begin. But Kennedy held his ground. The Soviet ships avoided the blocked area. Kennedy had won the showdown. This event became known as the Cuban missile crisis.

SUPREME COURT APPOINTMENTS

BRYON R. WHITE - 1962
ARTHUR J. GOLDBERG - 1962

The Nuclear Test-Ban Treaty went into effect on October 10, 1963.

Soon after the crisis, the Nuclear Test-Ban Treaty was signed. The United States, the Soviet Union, and Great Britain signed the treaty on August 5, 1963. Later, many other world nations agreed to it. The treaty limited most types of nuclear weapons testing.

TRAGEDY IN DALLAS

In 1963, Kennedy prepared for reelection. An important campaign stop was Texas. It was the home state of Vice President Johnson. On November 22, the Kennedys flew to Dallas, Texas. They arrived on the presidential airplane, Air Force One.

The Kennedys and the Johnsons then traveled through Dallas in convertible limousines. At about 12:30 PM, shots rang out. President Kennedy was hit in the head and the throat. He was quickly taken to a hospital. Just 30 minutes later, John F. Kennedy died.

President and Mrs. Kennedy arrived in Dallas after visiting San Antonio, Houston, and Fort Worth, Texas, the previous day.

On board Air Force One, Johnson took the oath of office. He became the thirty-sixth U.S. president. This was unlike any other presidential **inauguration** in U.S. history.

Lee Harvey Oswald was soon arrested for **assassinating** Kennedy. Oswald worked at the Texas School Book Depository building. The shots had been fired from there. However, Oswald denied his involvement.

Two days later, Oswald was being moved from one jail to another. A man named Jack Ruby shot and killed him. Ruby was sent to prison.

Lee Harvey Oswald

The entire world was shocked at the death of President Kennedy. People came to see his flag-draped coffin on November 24, 1963. It was laid out in the U.S. Capitol in Washington, D.C. Many thousands passed by to pay their last respects.

Leaders from 92 nations attended Kennedy's funeral the following day. President Kennedy was buried in Arlington National

Around 250,000 people visited the Capitol rotunda to honor President Kennedy before his funeral.

Cemetery near Washington, D.C. Mrs. Kennedy lit an eternal flame at her husband's grave.

John F. Kennedy served less than three years as president. He faced challenges in Germany, Vietnam, and at home. He also gave America a goal for future space travel. But, he is best remembered for successfully leading the country through the Cuban **missile** crisis.

After her death in 1994, Mrs. Kennedy was buried next to her husband in Arlington National Cemetery.

OFFICE OF THE PRESIDENT

BRANCHES OF GOVERNMENT

The U.S. government is divided into three branches. They are the executive, legislative, and judicial branches. This division is called a separation of powers. Each branch has some power over the others. This is called a system of checks and balances.

EXECUTIVE BRANCH

The executive branch enforces laws. It is made up of the president, the vice president, and the president's cabinet. The president represents the United States around the world. He or she oversees relations with other countries and signs treaties. The president signs bills into law and appoints officials and federal judges. He or she also leads the military and manages government workers.

LEGISLATIVE BRANCH

The legislative branch makes laws, maintains the military, and regulates trade. It also has the power to declare war. This branch consists of the Senate and the House of Representatives. Together, these two houses make up Congress. Each state has two senators. A state's population determines the number of representatives it has.

JUDICIAL BRANCH

The judicial branch interprets laws. It consists of district courts, courts of appeals, and the Supreme Court. District courts try cases. If a person disagrees with a trial's outcome, he or she may appeal. If the courts of appeals support the ruling, a person may appeal to the Supreme Court. The Supreme Court also makes sure that laws follow the U.S. Constitution.

QUALIFICATIONS FOR OFFICE

To be president, a person must meet three requirements. A candidate must be at least 35 years old and a natural-born U.S. citizen. He or she must also have lived in the United States for at least 14 years.

ELECTORAL COLLEGE

The U.S. presidential election is an indirect election. Voters from each state choose electors to represent them in the Electoral College. The number of electors from each state is based on population. Each elector has one electoral vote. Electors are pledged to cast their vote for the candidate who receives the highest number of popular votes in their state. A candidate must receive the majority of Electoral College votes to win.

TERM OF OFFICE

Each president may be elected to two four-year terms. Sometimes, a president may only be elected once. This happens if he or she served more than two years of the previous president's term.

The presidential election is held on the Tuesday after the first Monday in November. The president is sworn in on January 20 of the following year. At that time, he or she takes the oath of office:

I do solemnly swear (or affirm) that I will faithfully execute the office of President of the United States, and will to the best of my ability, preserve, protect and defend the Constitution of the United States.

Line of Succession

The Presidential Succession Act of 1947 defines who becomes president if the president cannot serve. The vice president is first in the line of succession. Next are the Speaker of the House and the President Pro Tempore of the Senate. If none of these individuals is able to serve, the office falls to the president's cabinet members. They would take office in the order in which each department was created:

Secretary of State

Secretary of the Treasury

Secretary of Defense

Attorney General

Secretary of the Interior

Secretary of Agriculture

Secretary of Commerce

Secretary of Labor

Secretary of Health and Human Services

Secretary of Housing and Urban Development

Secretary of Transportation

Secretary of Energy

Secretary of Education

Secretary of Veterans Affairs

Secretary of Homeland Security

BENEFITS

- While in office, the president receives a salary of $400,000 each year. He or she lives in the White House and has 24-hour Secret Service protection.

- The president may travel on a Boeing 747 jet called Air Force One. The airplane can accommodate 70 passengers. It has kitchens, a dining room, sleeping areas, and a conference room. It also has fully equipped offices with the latest communications systems. Air Force One can fly halfway around the world before needing to refuel. It can even refuel in flight!

- If the president wishes to travel by car, he or she uses Cadillac One. Cadillac One is a Cadillac Deville. It has been modified with heavy armor and communications systems. The president takes Cadillac One along when visiting other countries if secure transportation will be needed.

- The president also travels on a helicopter called Marine One. Like the presidential car, Marine One accompanies the president when traveling abroad if necessary.

- Sometimes, the president needs to get away and relax with family and friends. Camp David is the official presidential retreat. It is located in the cool, wooded mountains in Maryland. The U.S. Navy maintains the retreat, and the U.S. Marine Corps keeps it secure. The camp offers swimming, tennis, golf, and hiking.

- When the president leaves office, he or she receives Secret Service protection for ten more years. He or she also receives a yearly pension of $191,300 and funding for office space, supplies, and staff.

PRESIDENTS AND THEIR TERMS

PRESIDENT	PARTY	TOOK OFFICE	LEFT OFFICE	TERMS SERVED	VICE PRESIDENT
George Washington	None	April 30, 1789	March 4, 1797	Two	John Adams
John Adams	Federalist	March 4, 1797	March 4, 1801	One	Thomas Jefferson
Thomas Jefferson	Democratic-Republican	March 4, 1801	March 4, 1809	Two	Aaron Burr, George Clinton
James Madison	Democratic-Republican	March 4, 1809	March 4, 1817	Two	George Clinton, Elbridge Gerry
James Monroe	Democratic-Republican	March 4, 1817	March 4, 1825	Two	Daniel D. Tompkins
John Quincy Adams	Democratic-Republican	March 4, 1825	March 4, 1829	One	John C. Calhoun
Andrew Jackson	Democrat	March 4, 1829	March 4, 1837	Two	John C. Calhoun, Martin Van Buren
Martin Van Buren	Democrat	March 4, 1837	March 4, 1841	One	Richard M. Johnson
William H. Harrison	Whig	March 4, 1841	April 4, 1841	Died During First Term	John Tyler
John Tyler	Whig	April 6, 1841	March 4, 1845	Completed Harrison's Term	Office Vacant
James K. Polk	Democrat	March 4, 1845	March 4, 1849	One	George M. Dallas
Zachary Taylor	Whig	March 5, 1849	July 9, 1850	Died During First Term	Millard Fillmore

PRESIDENT	PARTY	TOOK OFFICE	LEFT OFFICE	TERMS SERVED	VICE PRESIDENT
Millard Fillmore	Whig	July 10, 1850	March 4, 1853	Completed Taylor's Term	Office Vacant
Franklin Pierce	Democrat	March 4, 1853	March 4, 1857	One	William R.D. King
James Buchanan	Democrat	March 4, 1857	March 4, 1861	One	John C. Breckinridge
Abraham Lincoln	Republican	March 4, 1861	April 15, 1865	Served One Term, Died During Second Term	Hannibal Hamlin, Andrew Johnson
Andrew Johnson	Democrat	April 15, 1865	March 4, 1869	Completed Lincoln's Second Term	Office Vacant
Ulysses S. Grant	Republican	March 4, 1869	March 4, 1877	Two	Schuyler Colfax, Henry Wilson
Rutherford B. Hayes	Republican	March 3, 1877	March 4, 1881	One	William A. Wheeler
James A. Garfield	Republican	March 4, 1881	September 19, 1881	Died During First Term	Chester Arthur
Chester Arthur	Republican	September 20, 1881	March 4, 1885	Completed Garfield's Term	Office Vacant
Grover Cleveland	Democrat	March 4, 1885	March 4, 1889	One	Thomas A. Hendricks
Benjamin Harrison	Republican	March 4, 1889	March 4, 1893	One	Levi P. Morton
Grover Cleveland	Democrat	March 4, 1893	March 4, 1897	One	Adlai E. Stevenson
William McKinley	Republican	March 4, 1897	September 14, 1901	Served One Term, Died During Second Term	Garret A. Hobart, Theodore Roosevelt

PRESIDENT	PARTY	TOOK OFFICE	LEFT OFFICE	TERMS SERVED	VICE PRESIDENT
Theodore Roosevelt	Republican	September 14, 1901	March 4, 1909	Completed McKinley's Second Term, Served One Term	Office Vacant, Charles Fairbanks
William Taft	Republican	March 4, 1909	March 4, 1913	One	James S. Sherman
Woodrow Wilson	Democrat	March 4, 1913	March 4, 1921	Two	Thomas R. Marshall
Warren G. Harding	Republican	March 4, 1921	August 2, 1923	Died During First Term	Calvin Coolidge
Calvin Coolidge	Republican	August 3, 1923	March 4, 1929	Completed Harding's Term, Served One Term	Office Vacant, Charles Dawes
Herbert Hoover	Republican	March 4, 1929	March 4, 1933	One	Charles Curtis
Franklin D. Roosevelt	Democrat	March 4, 1933	April 12, 1945	Served Three Terms, Died During Fourth Term	John Nance Garner, Henry A. Wallace, Harry S. Truman
Harry S. Truman	Democrat	April 12, 1945	January 20, 1953	Completed Roosevelt's Fourth Term, Served One Term	Office Vacant, Alben Barkley
Dwight D. Eisenhower	Republican	January 20, 1953	January 20, 1961	Two	Richard Nixon
John F. Kennedy	Democrat	January 20, 1961	November 22, 1963	Died During First Term	Lyndon B. Johnson
Lyndon B. Johnson	Democrat	November 22, 1963	January 20, 1969	Completed Kennedy's Term, Served One Term	Office Vacant, Hubert H. Humphrey
Richard Nixon	Republican	January 20, 1969	August 9, 1974	Completed First Term, Resigned During Second Term	Spiro T. Agnew, Gerald Ford

PRESIDENT	PARTY	TOOK OFFICE	LEFT OFFICE	TERMS SERVED	VICE PRESIDENT
Gerald Ford	Republican	August 9, 1974	January 20, 1977	Completed Nixon's Second Term	Nelson A. Rockefeller
Jimmy Carter	Democrat	January 20, 1977	January 20, 1981	One	Walter Mondale
Ronald Reagan	Republican	January 20, 1981	January 20, 1989	Two	George H.W. Bush
George H.W. Bush	Republican	January 20, 1989	January 20, 1993	One	Dan Quayle
Bill Clinton	Democrat	January 20, 1993	January 20, 2001	Two	Al Gore
George W. Bush	Republican	January 20, 2001	January 20, 2009	Two	Dick Cheney
Barack Obama	Democrat	January 20, 2009			Joe Biden

"Ask not what your country can do for you—ask what you can do for your country." John F. Kennedy

WRITE TO THE PRESIDENT

You may write to the president at:

The White House
1600 Pennsylvania Avenue NW
Washington, DC 20500

You may e-mail the president at:

comments@whitehouse.gov

GLOSSARY

Addison's disease - an illness marked by weight loss, low blood pressure, and a brown tint to the skin.

assassinate - to murder a very important person, usually for political reasons.

civil rights - the individual rights of a citizen, such as the right to vote or freedom of speech.

Cold War - a period of tension and hostility between the United States and its allies and the Soviet Union and its allies after World War II.

debate - a contest in which two sides argue for or against something.

Democrat - a member of the Democratic political party. Democrats believe in social change and strong government.

discrimination (dihs-krih-muh-NAY-shuhn) - unfair treatment based on factors such as a person's race, religion, or gender.

economic - of or relating to the way a nation uses its money, goods, and natural resources. Economics is the science of this.

inauguration (ih-naw-gyuh-RAY-shuhn) - a ceremony in which a person is sworn into office.

journalism - the collecting and editing of news to be presented in newspapers or magazines or over television or radio.

missile - a weapon that is thrown or projected to hit a target.

popular vote - the vote of the entire body of people with the right to vote.

Pulitzer Prize - an award established by journalist Joseph Pulitzer for accomplishments in journalism, literature, drama, and music.

Republican - a member of the Republican political party. Republicans are conservative and believe in small government.

running mate - a candidate running for a lower-rank position on an election ticket, especially the candidate for vice president.

segregation (seh-grih-GAY-shuhn) - the separation of an individual or a group from a larger group, especially by race.

stock market - a place where stocks and bonds, which represent parts of businesses, are bought and sold. Stocks are money that represent part of a business. People who purchase stocks can own part of the company.

World War II - from 1939 to 1945, fought in Europe, Asia, and Africa. Great Britain, France, the United States, the Soviet Union, and their allies were on one side. Germany, Italy, Japan, and their allies were on the other side.

WEB SITES

To learn more about John F. Kennedy, visit ABDO Publishing Company on the World Wide Web at **www.abdopublishing.com**. Web sites about John F. Kennedy are featured on our Book Links page. These links are routinely monitored and updated to provide the most current information available.

INDEX